To
Stacey

From
Dad
Xmas 2001

April May Dean-Linz

REFLECTIONS

by

April May Dean-Linz

All rights reserved.
Copyright © 2001 by April May Dean-Linz
No part of this book may be reproduced or transmitted in any form or by any means, electronic or mechanical, including photocopying, recording, or by any information storage and retrieval system without permission in writing from the publisher.

ISBN 0-9711049-0-5
Printed in the United States of America

Library of Congress Control Number 2001117212
Published by April May Dean-Linz

DEDICATION

First to God, it is only through Him that I was able to write. I give Him all the honor, and glory and praise.

*

To my husband David, I love you with all of my heart. You are such an encouragement to me. Thank you for sharing your life with me. I am privileged to be your wife and I pray that we have many years to walk closer, grow older, to laugh and to love life together.

*

To my baby boy, Matthew. You will never know how important you are to me. I may tell you every day that I love you, but I pray that my actions show you beyond a doubt. May you grow up to be healthy, happy and most of all to love the Lord. Mama loves you.

*

And to my mom, my best friend. I am so blessed to be your daughter. I appreciate you for all you have done for me and for helping me grow. I love you.

CONTENTS

A SPIRITUAL JOURNEY

Answers	11
Encouragement	12
Father	13
This Is My Cry	14
I'll Always Have You Lord	16
My Prayer Closet	18
Strength	19
Dean	20
Trials	22
A Package of Salvation	23
Brothers	24
Silent April May	27
Friends	28
untitled	29
Easter	30
Spring	31
Christ Only Always	32
With Jesus Christ	33

FROM THE HEART

Matthew	37
To Mom, With Love	38
Thanks Mom	39
Dear Grandmother, With Love	40
A Year Ago	41
A Magical Dream	42

A Dozen Roses	43
A Valentine Prayer	45
Love	46
Lover's Delight	47
Young Love	48
I Love You	49
Our Love	50
Control	51
A Second Look	52
He Took Me Away From You	53
A Broken Heart	54
Silence	55

JUST A THOUGHT

Our Future	59
I Want To Write	60
By the Sea	61
Winter	62
untitled	63
Colors	64
The Dreams	65
My Bedroom	66
Light	67
Life	68
Sometimes	69
Last Minute Exam	70
Always Fishing	72
Jonny Blue	73
Jingle Bells	74
Secrets	75
Memories	76

A SPIRITUAL JOURNEY

ANSWERS

Searching for some answers
To help me find my way
The Bible was my solution
I got on my knees to pray
Up to the Royal Master
I lift my spirits high
Listening to my Savior
I began to understand why
You came into my life Lord
And cleansed my soul from sin
From the blood that Your Son Jesus shed
So that I could be born again
As I continued to listen
To the story You had to tell
I felt nearer to You
My God, Emmanuel
Finding all my answers
I prayed again and again
Up to the Royal Master
Alleluia and Amen

AMD
10/21/90

ENCOURAGEMENT

Just in case you forgot today
Jesus Christ is on His way

He knows your troubles and your fears
He knows your worries and your tears

There may be times you don't feel right
And satan's lies give you a fright

Encouragement is what you need
The Holy Spirit will help succeed

Remind you that God is the best
Give Him your cares, He will take care of the rest

Just in case you forgot today
Jesus Christ is on His way

AMD
12/03/98

FATHER

Father, I adore You
Lay my life before You
Give You all the honor and the praise

Be ever with me
Guide my every footstep
Walk with me each and every day

You lived for me
You died for me
And then for me You rose

You are my discipler
My mentor, my teacher
My love that will not end

You are my Savior
My comforter, my healer
Jesus, You are my friend

AMD
03/24

THIS IS MY CRY

I want to know who and what and where and when
and how and why
Reaching out for Jesus - yes, this is my cry
I want to know who and what and where and when
and how and why
Giving all I've got for Him, I'm laying down my life

People are around me, each and every day
Looking for answers, looking for a way

Wanting to find reason, wanting to find truth
Wanting just to have the joy they see in me and you

I want to know who and what and where and when
and how and why
Reaching out for Jesus - yes, this is my cry
I want to know who and what and where and when
and how and why
Giving all I've got for Him, I'm laying down my life

Who are these people, what are their needs
Where is their heart Lord, and when will they see

How can I show them, why can't they see
My life as a witness, that You live in me

(cont.)

I want to know who and what and where and when
and how and why
Reaching out for Jesus - yes, this is my cry
I want to know who and what and where and when
and how and why
Giving all I've got for Him, I'm laying down my life

Daily let me worship, daily let me serve
Let Your light shine through me, to everyone on earth

Let them see Your glory, Let them see Your grace
Let them feel the power, to turn and seek Your face

I want to know who and what and where and when
and how and why
Reaching out for Jesus - yes, this is my cry
I want to know who and what and where and when
and how and why
Giving all I've got for Him, I'm laying down my life

AMD
10/04/96

I'LL ALWAYS HAVE YOU LORD

When my rainbow fades away
And the blue skies turn to gray
I'll always have You Lord

When the burdens never end
I can trust You as my friend
I'll always have You Lord

For whenever I need Your company
Or whenever I don't feel strong
You are always there beside me
Guiding me to where I belong

When I need a shoulder to cry on
When I need to hold Your hand
All I have to do is ask You
And You give to my demand

When the fire inside me dies
And the pain inside me cries
I'll always have You Lord

When I have a broken heart
You can fix it part by part
I'll always have You Lord

(cont.)

Lord I know I've not been faithful
In the commands You gave to me
When I ask for Your forgiveness
You say "My child, you are set free"

My devotions are a shamble
My daily prayers to You are few
But the ones I send Your way Lord
Every one of them is true

When my life is filled with fears
And I can't hold back the tears
I'll always have You Lord

When I'm tired of playing this game
Only myself I have to blame
I'll always have You Lord

For I know not why You love me
And I don't know what I've done
But I know that You have promised
To be my only one

I'll always have You Lord
I'll always have You Lord
I'll always have You Lord

AMD
original 01/17/94
revised 03/15/01

MY PRAYER CLOSET

As I enter in my prayer closet
I'm not sure what to say
So I get down on my knees
And I quietly start to pray
"Dear God" I say, I'm thankful
For the things You've done through me
For the blessings You have given
For Your Son who set me free
For my church that I can grow with
For my family and my friends
For Your undivided attention
For Your love that never ends
For all my answered prayers
For the Bible, Your Holy Word
For the good things, I will praise You
For the bad, I'll praise You more
I know indeed without You
That I wouldn't have a chance
Thank you God in heaven
For giving me another glance

AMD
01/05/93

STRENGTH

Sunday evening
I feel so blue
For a moment
I lost contact with You

I need Your strength Lord
I need to know
That You're here with me
While I'm feeling low

I made a mistake God
And I'm paying the cost
But with Your forgiveness
I won't stay lost

Close to me forever
I pray to Thy name
And I know that You love me
I can feel Your strength

AMD
11/90

DEAN

A little boy
His name is Dean
A gift from God
A mothers dream

Nine months
He finally came
The doctors said
He's not the same

You worried and prayed
And shed some tears
Filled with confusion,
Sadness and fears

You don't understand
How this could be
How did this happen
O Lord, Why me

This little boy
A gift from You
How can we help him
What can we do

(cont.)

It may take him longer
To do little things
But with every attempt
He gives you a grin

He laughs and smiles
He giggles and cries
He coo's and awe's
He brightens our lives

Every day
We learn and grow
Into Your hands
Dear Lord we know

A little boy
His name is Dean
A gift from God
A mothers dream

* Dedicated to Dean Charles Mihailov

AMDL
09/08/99

TRIALS

Through all trials and worries
I sometimes don't understand
And I often feel lonely
Though You have the upper hand

I'm thankful You are beside me
To show me that You are gracious
Always a step ahead
I can feel Your precious patience

My prayers are being lifted
They come straight from the heart
To keep You in control Lord
And to give You every part

When I stop walking with You
I feel alone and afraid
When I don't lean on You
But the choices I have made

I know it is essential
To keep You close to me
To give You all my burdens
To set my spirit free

Forgive me of my sins Lord
And release them from my soul
To be filled with Your riches
And glory to become whole

AMD
04/15/93

A PACKAGE OF SALVATION

When you ask the Lord to be your Savior, He will give you a package of salvation. Included is a one-way ticket to heaven. No refunds, exchanges or expiration date. Just a reservation for happiness and joy. A gift certificate for eternal life which comes fully loaded with love, friendship, peace and true riches. A personal invitation to dine with the Master at the buffet of humbleness, meekness and gentleness. A double coupon for contentment and a free pass for answers to prayers. This package is available to the public and there is no shipping and handling fee. To receive your package of salvation, simply get down on your knees and ask the Lord to come into your life and be your personal Savior.

AMD
07/22/93

BROTHERS

Said one brother to another
Have you heard about the Lord
Have you heard about His promise
Have you heard about His Word

Said the other to this brother
I just don't have time to see
What the Lord has to offer
Or what He has given me

Said the brother to the other
Make wise of your time spent
You need to learn of the Master
You need to learn to repent

Repent said this brother
Is that some kind of prayer
If it is, well my brother
I really don't give a care

Said the brother to the other
How could you not give a care
If it wasn't for the Master
Brother, you wouldn't be here

(cont.)

Repent is nothing more
Than giving to God your sins
Asking Him for forgiveness
Then praying and starting again

A little of the scriptures
Will set you heart in motion
It will give you major guidance
In your walk and your devotion

My brother God is awesome
He's done wonders in my life
He has blessed me with a family
He has given me a beautiful wife

Said one brother to another
Are you starting to understand
Life can be so much richer
If you only hold Gods hand

My brother the Christian life
Is the life that can't be beat
It's a life that's full of riches
It's a life that is sweet

The "real world" can't come close
To the treasures God has given
It can't even scratch the surface
It's not the life to be living

(cont.)

So brother pray with me
Let me help you to the Lord
Let Him fill you with His glory
Let Him fill you with His Word

Said the other to this brother
Thanks for taking out the time
Thanks for showing me the Savior
And for letting Him be mine

Said the brother to the other
Just remember God's your friend
And remember to rely on Him
He will be with you till the end

AMD
08/03/92

SILENT APRIL MAY

Sitting by the ocean
Was silent April May
Watching waves come to shore
Washing the sand away

As she stares straight ahead
Not one word to be spoken
Tears begin to fall
Her heart had just been broken

She thinks of the Mighty One
Who gave and took her love away
She stops the tears from falling
And then begins to pray

Thanking Him for what He's done
She now understands why
She is being looked over
By God's angels from the sky

AMD
1990

FRIENDS

Tied down with many burdens
More than you can hold
Stressed from all the worry
You remain trying to be bold
A hand is reaching out to you
Although you turn away
They ask if they can help
But you don't know what to say
If you answer "yes"
You may let go and cry
If you answer "no"
Deep inside you may have lied
Not knowing where to turn
You sit there is despair
Even if they are out there
And you know that they care
A friend is there and wants to help
But you just won't let him in
When they saw that you were hurting
They hoped to ease the pain
You've slowly started talking
And the tears begin to pour
Your friend is the reassurance
That you can talk some more

(cont.)

Soon your burdens you have emptied
And let out in the open
Appreciative of your friend
And the time that they have given
No one can face life alone
That's what friends are for
They were given to us by God
Because He's been there before

AMD
05/30/92

untitled

I thank
the Lord
for His
Word that
teaches
me rules. Rules of good, rules of
bad, and rules to tell the truth.
Rules that say..."honor thy father
and thy mother" in everything you
do. Be
thankful
for them;
for they
are
thankful
for you.
Obey these
rules and
become
right, and
don't
forget to
pray each
night.
Amen.

AMD
05/29/92

EASTER

From a manger to a cross, from the cross to the tomb, from the tomb to heaven. What a wonderful picture of Christ's love for us.

He could have gone against His Father's will and let each of us go astray. But He didn't! He loved us enough to give His life, to provide payment for our sins. And He is continuously loving us, for the tomb is empty, He has risen.

This and every Easter, let us not reflect on pink rabbits, hiding eggs or eating chocolate. Those artificial traditions are only that...artificial. Let our thoughts and our hearts reflect upon the precious sacrifices Jesus made for each and every one of us. For He came that we may have life and have it more abundantly. Praise God.

Christ died for our sins according to the scriptures. And that He was buried and that He rose again, the third day, according to the scriptures.
                                II Corinthians 15:3-4

AMD
04/96

SPRING

She sat by the window
And looked at the sky
Watching and waiting
As birds flew by
What a beautiful sight
Though she wanted to cry

She didn't know the Father
That gave her these things
The sky with clouds
The birds with wings
Or the grass that is green
And grows in the spring

That day she had learned
What a blessing it was
That God gave her life
And all just because
He is our Master
Each one of us He loves

AMD
02/03/89

CHRIST ONLY ALWAYS

Christ only always
Never in second place
He is my Master
He is my King
The ultimate believer
The ultimate achiever
I bow down before thee
Give praise to thy name
He who's beside me
Loveth and guideth me
Protect and watch over me
All day through the night
Christ only always
Never in second place
He is my Master
He is my King
His kingdom be glorified
Until the day I die
And then forever more
I'll give thee my love
Christ only always
Never in second place
He is my Master
He is my King

AMD
08/92

WITH JESUS CHRIST

With Jesus Christ we have it all
And with His love we'll have a ball
He is always there when we call
To pick us up when we fall
Our faith in Him is often small
But His gifts to us could fill a mall
He provides a path straight as a hall
Though at the end there is no wall
To climb life's mountain is sometimes tall
But with Jesus Christ we'll have it all

AMD
02/12/93

FROM THE HEART

MATTHEW

Matthew, Matthew
My sweet baby boy
You bring me sunshine
And you bring me joy

I want to hold this moment
And I know the memories will last
But my baby you're growing so quickly
And time is going by fast

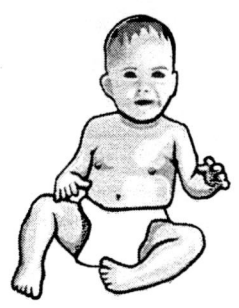

AMDL
03/17/01

TO MOM, WITH LOVE

A friend indeed
She is so true
Always helping
When I'm feeling blue
She understands
My problems and fears
When they occur
She is near
Her devotion is strong
With a pleasant smile
Just for me
She would walk a mile
Appreciation and love
To her I shall give
Together as friends
We'll grow and we'll live
If up to me
I would choose no other
Because God granted me
The greatest mother

AMD
01/14/91

THANKS MOM

You wash the clothes
And do the dishes
Try and answer
To all our wishes
Pick up the phone
Though it's the wrong number
Stack the papers
That are in a fumble
Shake the rugs
And mop the floors
Get up and close
The opened doors
Duane is home
Off the road
But in the semi
Is another load
Fixing supper
Is quite a job
Burn your hand
On the hot knob
You're tuckered out
And ready for bed
You take two aspirin
For your head
Mother of the year award
You certainly deserve
Hope that we didn't
Get on your nerves
Thanks mom!

AMD

DEAR GRANDMOTHER, WITH LOVE

I never got the chance to say
How much you meant to me
But in the things I did for you
I tried to let you see
No one could replace
Your tender love and care
When I needed a friendly laugh or hug
You were always there
Today brought tears and sorrow
For we had to say good-bye
Until our next reunion
In our home above the sky
We'll talk and chat about the times
You gave joy to me
About when I was little
And you bounced me on your knee
I know you are at peace now
But it's hard to let you go
I try to hold back the tears
But they are going to flow
Dear grandmother how I love you
And I have right from the start
You will always be so special
And stay close within my heart

* In loving memory of Pauline B. Leonard

AMD
02/26/91

A YEAR AGO

A year ago today she died
And on my pillow today I cried
Still asking questions, not understanding why
A year ago today she died

The family is still healing
Few of the answers revealing
"Just trust in God" they say to us
Yes indeed - He has our trust

I go to the grave and say a prayer
Somehow, I think, she knows I'm there
Granddad still can't bare to go
When he can - only God knows

Duane wants to in his heart
But his emotions stop his start
The rest of the family visits too
Though deep inside feeling blue

Yes, a year ago today she died
And again I will cry
I love her so, it's plain to see
Grandmother I love you, love always, me

AMD
02/23/92

A MAGICAL DREAM

Rebecca and Joe
A magical dream
Binded together
Forever it seems
Their love so strong
So pure, so true
Intuned with God
Indeed a value
More previous than gold
No riches can buy
Like the stars in the night
Their love brightens the sky
Love like this
Is special but few
Made by God
This one is true

AMD
11/09/90 original
12/08/98 revised

A DOZEN ROSES

One rose to say
I love you
One rose to say
I care
One rose to say
I need you
One rose to say
I'll be there
One rose to say
You're special
One rose to say
You're unique
One rose to say
You're beautiful
One rose to say
You're sweet
One rose to say
You're important
One rose to say
You're devine
One rose to say
Forever
One rose to say
You're mine
So here's a dozen roses
Each with a different note
Each with a different message
With love to you I devote

AMD

A VALENTINE PRAYER

Matchmaker, matchmaker
Please make me a match
Please find me a find
Please catch me a catch

Cupid my friend
Get the show on the road
But a little advice
I'm not kissing a toad

The dating game
Lots of fun I expect
At the end of the night
I'm stuck with the check

The love connection
Where dreams become real
When I won the grand prize
My date was...a seal

I'll place an ad
In today's morning news
Stated -- valentine needed
Now how can I lose

(cont.)

It's the 90's they say
Computer datings around
A note on the screen
All systems are down

Oh well - I guess
I'll just have to wait
But with my luck
I know he'll be late

LOVE

Love is something soft
Flowing through the air

Love is something special
That two people share

Love is something beautiful
Which words cannot describe

Love is something honest
The way we feel inside

AMD

LOVER'S DELIGHT

A wish, a kiss, a whistle too
As he calls back, I love you
A tap, a touch, then arm in arm
He surprises you with his charm

First the phone call
The dates at night
I guess it's called
Lover's delight

AMD

YOUNG LOVE

I feel happy
When you are near
I feel empty
When you aren't here

I think of you
Night and day
You are the one
I hope and pray

As time goes by
I wish I was
With you forever
And always because

I want to hold you
Close to me
Enjoy your time
And company

Please say you love me
And tell me it's true
We will be together
Because...I love you

AMD

I LOVE YOU

You're someone special
Through and through
Someone to spend time with
And care for too

When I'm with you
During the day
I want to say I love you
But I don't know the way

Sharing the feelings
That I hide
Expressing my thoughts
Deep from inside

So if the way I feel
Is really true
Now I am saying
I love you

AMD
02/02/89

OUR LOVE

The day I saw him
We fell in love

A love as strong
As the stars above

He's there for me
When I'm feeling sad

He's there for me
When I'm feeling glad

He's there for me
To love and hold

Our love will continue
As we grow old

AMD

CONTROL

You made me feel grief
You made me feel pain
By using you
I had nothing to gain

I thought you would help
Get rid of my worries
I thought you could help
But you made me discouraged

I didn't know how powerful
You could be
Until you started taking
Control of me

The strength I needed
To get you away
Just the word "no"
I had to say

Now you are gone
And I am free
And I am happy
Like I wanted to be

AMD
02/09/89

A SECOND LOOK

I don't need them
I want to be free
If I don't need them
They won't need me

I tried them before
And they didn't work
I found out that
I was being a jerk

Three days in the hospital
Is all it took
Now I am taking
A second look

Today there has been
Another change
Things in my life
I have to rearrange

I need to talk to someone
But I don't know who
Someone to depend on
That is unlike you

Wishing and hoping
Is all it took
Now I am taking
A second look

AMD

HE TOOK ME AWAY FROM YOU

He took me away from you
Saved me from a lot of pain
He took me way from you
Though I turned back once again

And He said...come follow Me
Walk right in my path
A path as straight as can be
I'll hold your hand, come follow Me

Then I thought once
Then twice again
Of who was my true
And faithful friend

I followed Him
And now I'm on that path
I thank You dear Lord Jesus
Now I'm home at last

AMD
1989

A BROKEN HEART

For the love of both of us
It was going very far
But now that it is over
I have a broken heart

If it could be different
Just maybe things could change
And to improve the distance
With no one left to blame

Yet I love you dearly
It doesn't seem so real
How I can express myself
Truly how I feel

AMD

SILENCE

We sleep in silence through the night
Not one word to be spoken
Splitting apart further now
Our hearts becoming broken

Looking at each other
We both can feel the pain
Through another day now
The silence stays the same

Suddenly we begin to speak
Then into another fight
But now the day is over
And not another silent night

AMD
1987

JUST A THOUGHT

OUR FUTURE

Kids shooting kids
It's out of control
Everyone has "rights"
But no one follows the rules

What's going on
The questions been asked
Finger's get pointed
And the blame gets passed

It takes people to stand up
It takes people to talk
It takes people to teach
It takes people to walk

It starts with respect
And it starts with compassion
We need to make effort
We need to take action

Our future is at stake
Our kids need us now
Lets get the job done
Don't ask why - but how

AMDL
03/17/01

I WANT TO WRITE

I want to write
And give you my words
Spell out my thoughts
You may have heard

I want to write
Jot down my ideas
Empty my brain
And pencil my feelings

I want to write
On the paper with ink
With a little description
Let you know what I think

AMDL
03/17/01

BY THE SEA

Sitting by the sea
Just you and me
We will be together
Forever and ever
Sitting by the sea

AMD

WINTER

Leaves are changing
In the fall
Different colors
One in all

Grass is growing
Brown and thin
The trees grow bare
As winter begins

The snow is coming
Cold as can be
A sight as pretty
As a sight to see

AMD

untitled

Like the stars up in the sky
There's a sparkle in your eye

Like the clouds up above
In our hearts there is love

Like the castle on the hill
When there's a way, there's a will

Like the diamond on the ace
I'll stand by you in any place

AMD

COLORS

Red is for the apples
Falling from the trees

Yellow is the color
Of little bumble bees

Green is for the clover
Growing in the field

Blue is for the sky
As far as you can see

AMD

THE DREAMS

I was playing around. I was playing down town. Now I can say that it will be a sunny day. For I had a dream last night. And you say that it's all right dreaming a dream. So think about it, yes you. Just think about it. I will too. Oh the dream will last, please don't go so fast. I can't wait to see the dreams. Yes you say my dreams won't end till May. And you say it's right to dream a dream. So I'll go right ahead dreaming my dreams. But you say my dreams won't end till May. Because you haven't dreamed them. Oh my dreams.

* This was written when I was ten years old. If it doesn't make any sense, that is the reason why.

AMD
10/82

MY BEDROOM

My bedroom is black. No walls. No furniture.

It has no windows, black posters on the floor.

The floor is black and my bedroom is a mess.

No ceiling. A black tv and phone. Now we're

staying at my moms' friends house and

I'm sleeping in the living room.

* This was written when I was ten. My family had just been through losing our house to a fire, and this is what I wrote for a language assignment.

AMD
03/31/82

LIGHT

The light is shining brightly
Through the clouds above
The trees are swaying by the pond
Filled with ducks and doves

The water is flowing clearly
In the gentle stream
The breeze is soft and cool
As I sit and dream

My thoughts begin to wonder
Through the thick and thin
And the day continues
As the light soon dims

* This was written around the age of ten.

AMD

LIFE

Life is the flower
Growing in the field

Life is the car
At a sign which says yield

Life is a balloon
Flowing in the wind

Life is a baby
Who's life will soon begin

Life is being happy
And carefree in your days

Life is knowing today
And living in it's ways

Living
In
Free
Emotion

* This was written at a very young age.

AMD

SOMETIMES

Sometimes we look
For things that are right here
Sometimes we hide
The things we should share

Sometimes we say
Things not to be said
Sometimes we take steps
But don't get ahead

Sometimes we make it
All of the time
But even if you don't
You'll make it sometimes

AMD
02/02/89

LAST MINUTE EXAM

An hour of writing
There's no time to rest
An hour of study
For tomorrow's the test

Caffeine and sugar
The practical way
Cram all night
A definite "A"

Filling my brain
With things to be learned
An hour till class
I'm totally burned

Figures and numbers
And symbols combined
No more equations
I'm blowing my mind

Eight o'clock in the morning
The sound of the bell
Here comes the exam
I'm sure to do well

What are these problems
My uncertain thought
To solve them correctly
I just plain forgot

(cont.)

Five minutes remaining
I won't be done
Not even a chance
I'm only on number one

Time is up
She yells from her seat
Pass them forward
You better not cheat

Looking them over
And grading them all
She watches me
As I head for the hall

I'm back to my room
My alarm starts to scream
Lucky for me
This was only a dream

AMD
revised 03/05/01

ALWAYS FISHING

Life is sweet
Always wishing
When you're in a boat
Always fishing
The sport is great
I love it so
The name of the fish
I really don't know
Every day
You catch a few
Some are old
Some are new
Here's a catch
You just can't miss
A sweet and honest
Little kiss

AMD

JONNY BLUE

Jonny blue of the sea
Can I come swim with thee
Share the water in the sun
For tomorrow there my be none

Jonny blue of the sea
Won't you please answer me
The sun will soon fade away
And may not come another day

Jonny blue of the sea
Waves come up one, two, three
You are so quiet without a sound
Not one word to be found

Jonny blue of the sea
You're not a her nor a he
Jonny blue you are so free
Jonny blue you are the sea

AMD

JINGLE BELLS

Jingle Bells, Jingle Bells
Ring, ring, ring
Joy to the world
The children sing

Now Dasher, Dancer, Rudolph too
Merry Christmas to all
And Merry Christmas
To you

AMD

SECRETS

Secrets in the springtime
Secrets in the fall
Secrets to be kept private
Every one in all

Secrets of love and passion
Secrets of anger and hate
Secrets that will determine
Whether to tell or wait

AMD

MEMORIES

Memories are so special
To hold and keep inside
But still they can hurt you
If you run and hide

Keep them close to you
And never let them leave
Someday what you recall
You may not believe

AMD

INDEX

A Broken Heart	54
A Dozen Roses	45
A Magical Dream	42
A Package of Salvation	23
A Second Look	52
A Valentine Prayer	43
A Year Ago	41
Always Fishing	71
Answers	11
Brothers	24
By the Sea	61
Christ Only Always	33
Colors	62
Control	51
Dean	20
Dear Grandmother, With Love	40
Easter	31
Encouragement	12
Father	13
Friends	28
He Took Me Away From You	53
I'll Always Have You Lord	16
I Love You	49
I Want To Write	60
Jingle Bells	73
Jonny Blue	72
Last Minute Exam	69
Life	68
Light	67
Love	46
Lovers' Delight	47
Matthew	37

Memories	67
My Bedroom	66
My Prayer Closet	18
Our Future	59
Our Love	50
Secrets	75
Silence	55
Silent April May	27
Sometimes	74
Spring	32
Strength	19
Thanks Mom	39
The Dreams	65
This Is My Cry	14
To Mom, With Love	38
Trials	22
Untitled	30
Untitled	63
Winter	62
With Jesus Christ	34
Young Love	38

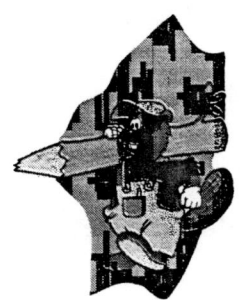

A special thank you to my family, God has truly blessed me with your love.

David Linz, Matthew

Mary & Duane Leonard

Bruce & Rosemary Dean

Don & Java Dean, Doug, Tai, Brittny

Joe & Beckie Bradley, Corey, David

Debby Humes, Darin, Jeff, Kristen, Steve Humes

Phil & Christy Ferry, Glenn

Doug & Amy Beck, Brandon, Shannon, Bradley, Dillon

Sherry Alford, Nathaniel

Joe & Peggy Linz

Steve Linz

Mary Truax, Mary Cogley, June Hough